Fish Life Cycle

Life Cycles of Living Things

Tracy Vonder Brink

Table of Contents

A Starfish Book

SEAHORSE PUBLISHING

Teaching Tips for Caregivers:

As a caregiver, you can help your child succeed in school by giving them a strong foundation in language and literacy skills and a desire to learn to read.

This book helps children grow by letting them practice reading skills.

Reading for pleasure and interest will help your child to develop reading skills and will give your child the opportunity to practice these skills in meaningful ways.

- Encourage your child to read on her own at home
- Encourage your child to practice reading aloud
- Encourage activities that require reading
- Establish a reading time
- Talk with your child
- Give your child writing materials

Teaching Tips for Teachers:

Research shows that one of the best ways for students to learn a new topic is to read about it.

Before Reading

- Read the "Words to Know" and discuss the meaning of each word.
- Read the back cover to see what the book is about.

During Reading

- When a student gets to a word that is unknown, ask them to look at the rest of the sentence to find clues to help with the meaning of the unknown word.
- Ask the student to write down any pages of the book that were confusing to them.

After Reading

- Discuss the main idea of the book.
- Ask students to give one detail that they learned in the book by showing a text dependent answer from the book.

Fish Life Cycle

All living things are born.

They grow to be adults.

We call these changes a life cycle.

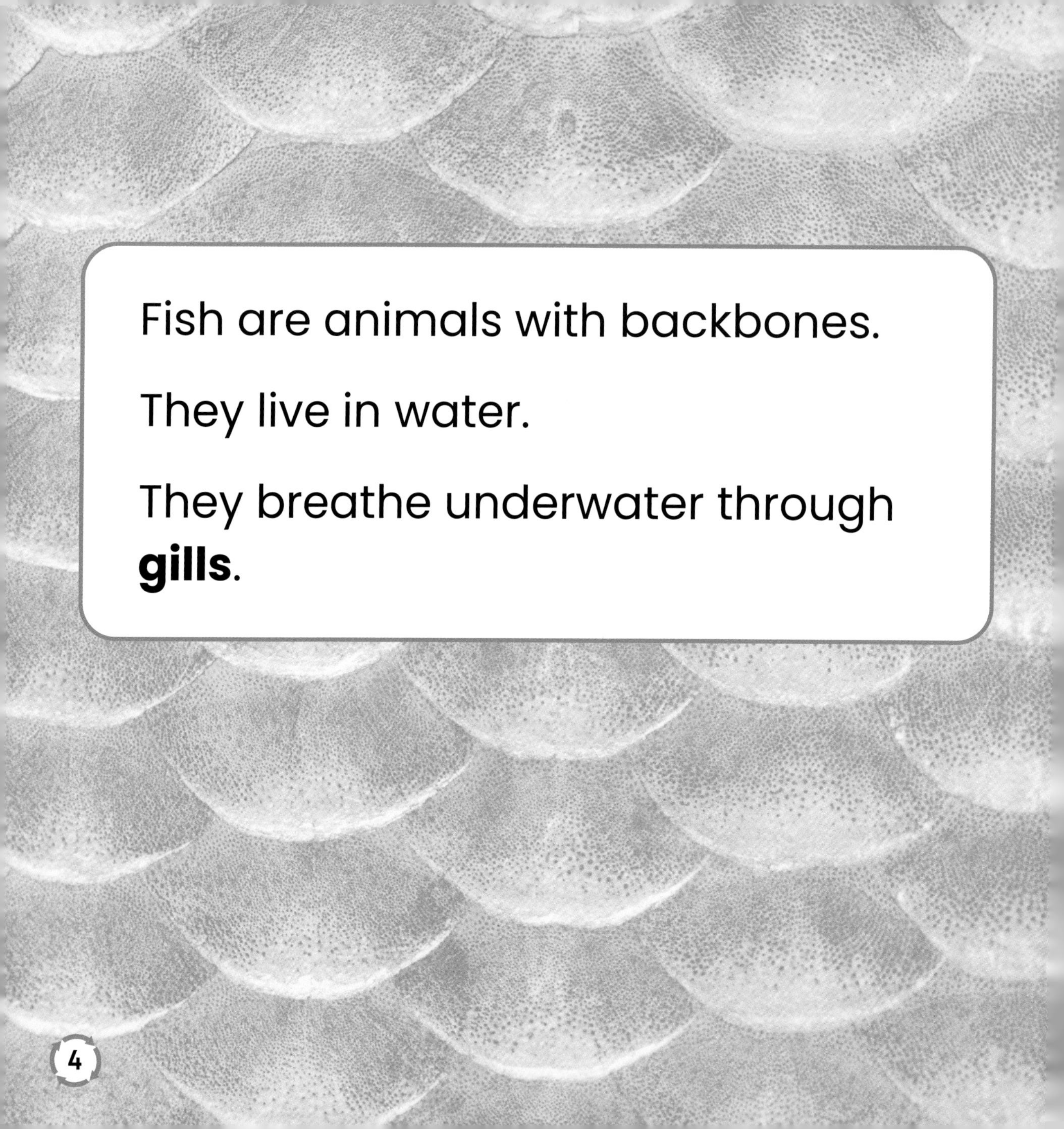

Fish are animals with backbones.

They live in water.

They breathe underwater through **gills**.

Fish have fins that help them move through the water.

A fish's life cycle begins with an egg.

An **embryo** grows inside.

Fish lay many eggs at a time. Some lay thousands.

The embryo becomes a **larva**.

The larva hatches from the egg.

The larva eats from a yolk sac attached to its body.

Some kinds of fish keep the yolk sac for a few days.

Some keep it for a few weeks.

Some fry eat tiny water plants and insects.

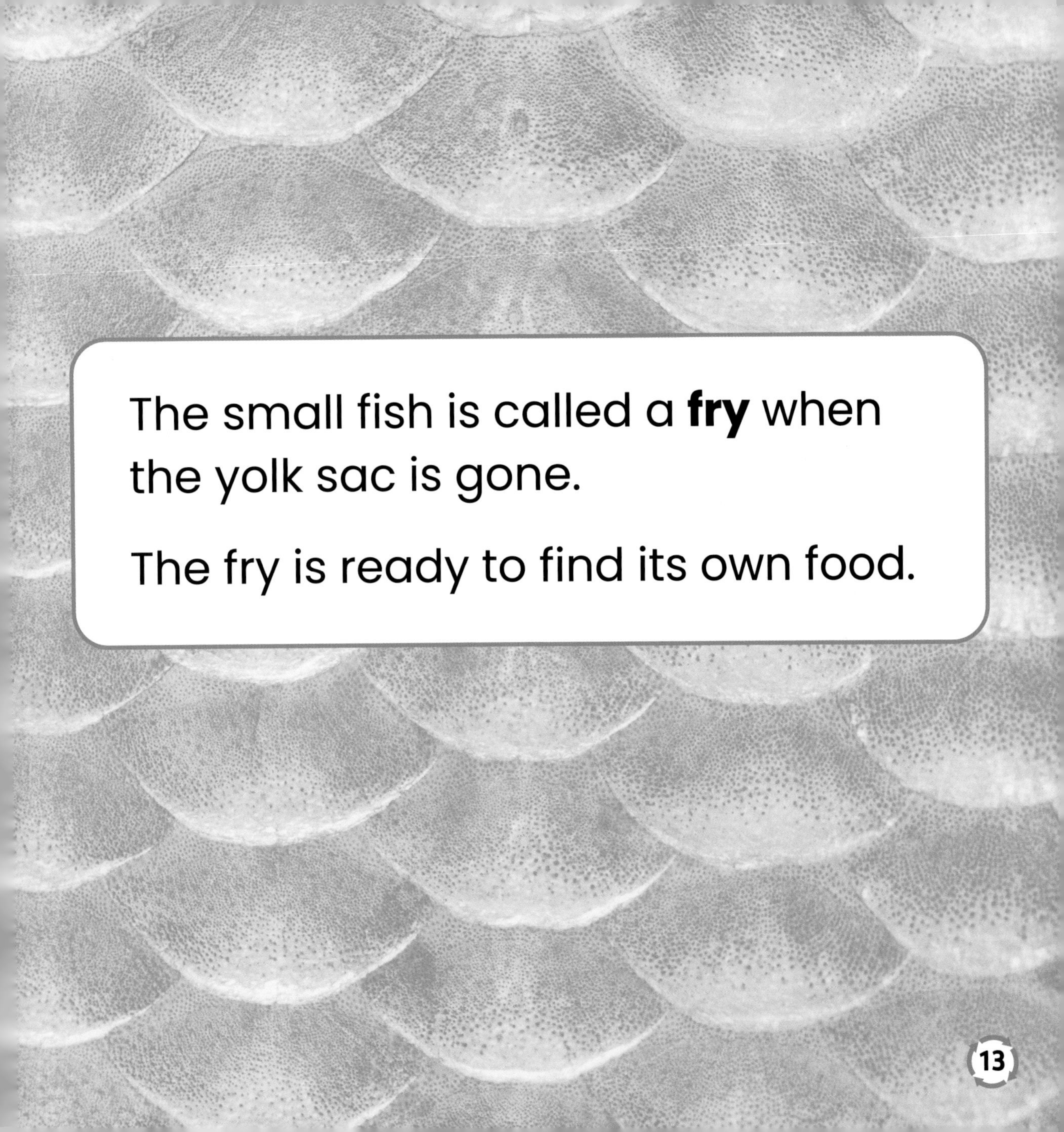

The small fish is called a **fry** when the yolk sac is gone.

The fry is ready to find its own food.

The fry becomes a **juvenile**.

The juvenile looks like a small adult fish.

But it cannot yet have babies of its own.

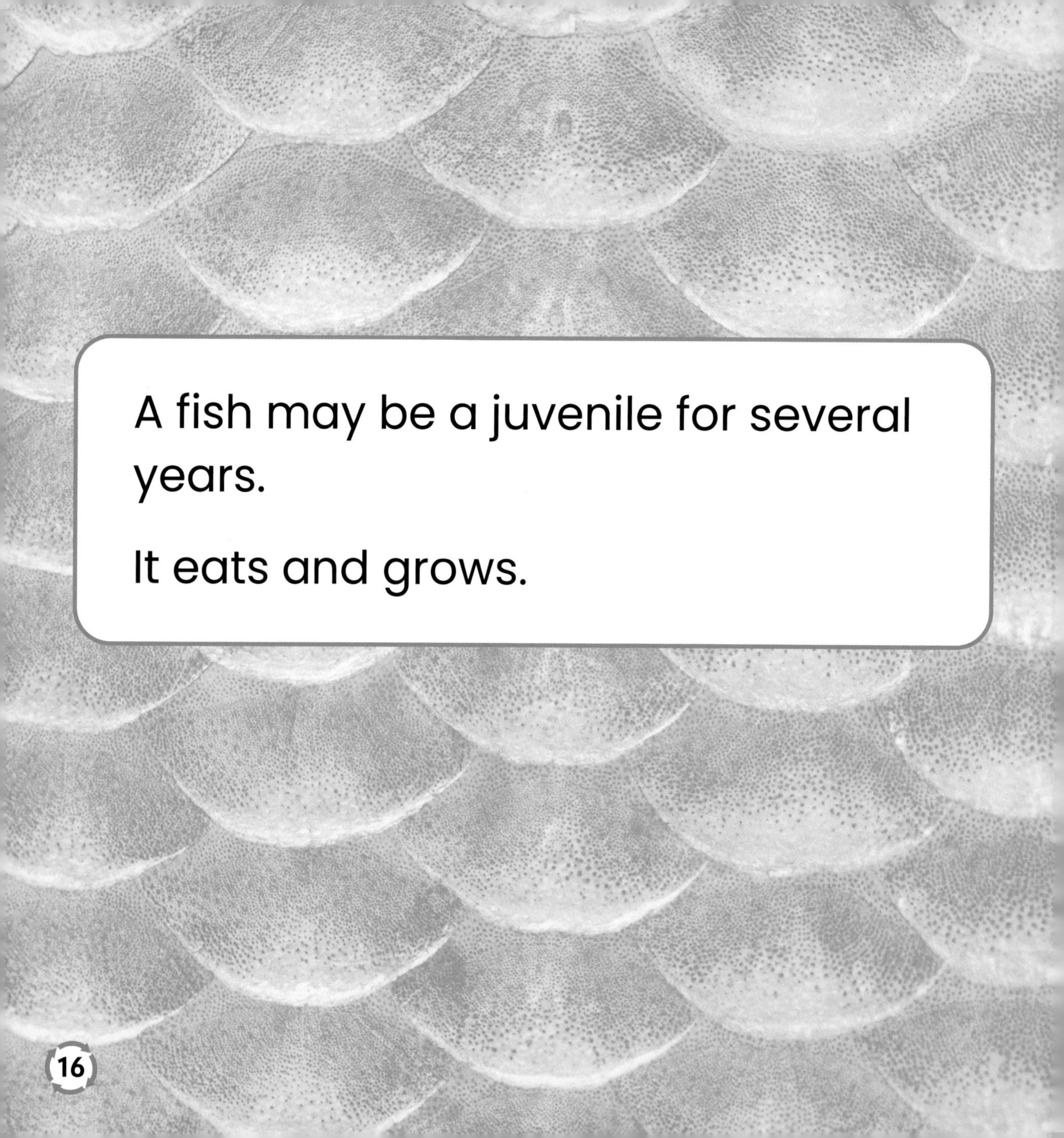

A fish may be a juvenile for several years.

It eats and grows.

The juvenile becomes an adult.

Adults are able to **spawn**.

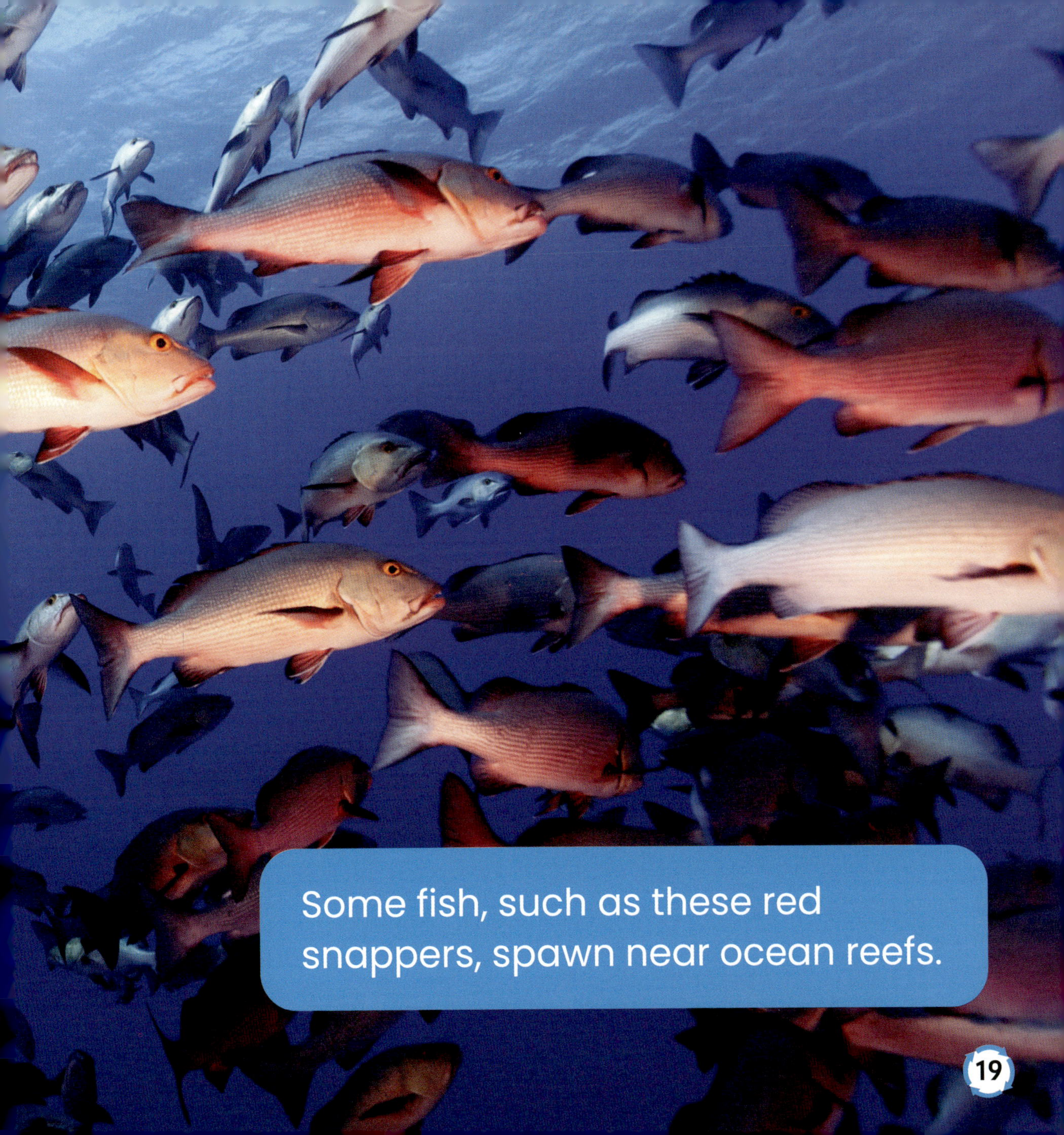

Some fish, such as these red snappers, spawn near ocean reefs.

The female fish lays eggs.

The life cycle begins again.

Words to Know

embryo (EM-bree-oh): a living creature in the earliest stage of development, before it is hatched or born

fry (frye): the stage of a young fish's life when it eats on its own and not from its yolk sac

gills (gilz): body parts near the mouth in fish and other living creatures that allow them to breathe underwater

juvenile (JOO-vuh-nile): a young living creature that has not yet reached its adult form

larva (LAHR-vuh): a stage in the development of many living creatures that happens between birth or hatching and before adulthood

spawn (spawn): to produce young

Index

Comprehension Questions

1. A fish's life cycle begins with
a. gills. **b.** an egg. **c.** a larva.

2. A fry
a. eats from a yolk sac.
b. is fed by its parents.
c. finds food on its own.

3. A juvenile fish cannot
a. find food on its own.
b. swim fast.
c. have its own babies.

4. True or false: Fish breathe underwater through lungs.

5. True or false: A juvenile fish looks like a small adult fish.

Answers
1. b 2. c 3. c 4. False 5. True

About the Author

Tracy Vonder Brink loves true stories and facts. She has written more than twenty books for kids and is a contributing editor for three children's science magazines. Tracy lives in Cincinnati, Ohio, with her husband, two daughters, and two rescue dogs.

Written by: Tracy Vonder Brink
Design by: Bobbie Houser
Editor: Kim Thompson

Library of Congress PCN Data
Fish Life Cycle / Tracy Vonder Brink
Life Cycles of Living Things
ISBN 978-1-63897-454-3 (hard cover)
ISBN 978-1-63897-569-4 (paperback)
ISBN 978-1-63897-684-4 (EPUB)
ISBN 978-1-63897-799-5 (eBook)
Library of Congress Control Number: 2021953376

Printed in the United States of America.

Photographs:
t = Top, b = Bottom, c = Center, l = Left, r = Right

Shutterstock: viper345: cover tl; SeraphP: cover tr; Alex Stemmers: cover b; Kazakova Maryia: p. 3; Pix Box: p. 5; Eric Lemar: pp. 6-7; HelloRF Zcool: p. 9; Zykov_ Vladimir: p. 11; Toxotes Hun-Gabor Horvath: p. 12; Dennis Jacobsen: p. 15; Laura Dts: p. 17; Pete Niesen: pp. 18-19; Dawinee Theetrakool: p. 20

Seahorse Publishing Company
www.seahorsepub.com

Published in the United States
Seahorse Publishing
PO Box 771325
Coral Springs, FL 33077

SEAHORSE PUBLISHING